Cooking in Hampshire
Past and Present

KATE EASLEA

**PAUL CAVE
PUBLICATIONS**
LTD

£1

Cover picture: Chilcomb, near Winchester (John Taverner)

Published: November, 1973
1st Re-print: January, 1974
2nd Re-print: March, 1974
3rd Re-print: May, 1974
4th Re-print: December, 1974
5th Re-print: February, 1975
6th Re-print: September, 1976
7th Re-print: September, 1977
8th Re-print: February, 1979
and several times later.
Revised edition: November, 1990

ISBN   0-86146-079-0

PREFACE

The standard and variety of cooking in Hampshire can compare very favourably with those in other counties of Great Britain, but for too many years have remained in the background.

I recently discovered this when asked by Solent Radio to suggest a 'typical Hampshire' recipe for a programme on Rural Home Economics in this county. This proved harder than anticipated as I could find very few cookery books with even regional dishes let alone a Hampshire one.

I decided from that moment to remedy this omission and the result is this little book with a collection of old and new recipes, all with a Hampshire flavour. I have been ably assisted in my research by many members of the Hampshire Women's Institutes and friends who I have met in the course of my work around the villages in the county. Some very old recipes were uncovered for me by the staff of the Department of Home Economics, Elizabeth Gaskell College of Education, Manchester. You will find some included in my book after modification and adaptation.

Hampshire is in most part a very fertile county with rich farming land. Pig farming has been widespread for many years, and it is also famous for strawberries and the watercress grown in the beautiful river valleys. So I have endeavoured to include a number of recipes which use these products.

All the recipes have been tested and are not difficult to cook and serve, neither are they extravagant or expensive.

I wish all who buy this book plenty of fun and much success with their 'Cooking in Hampshire'.

Kate Easlea

Previous Head of Rural Home Economics

Hampshire College of Agriculture

Sparsholt, Winchester, Hants.

P.S. I have now revised this book and have included some new recipes which I feel you will enjoy.

All recipes are for four portions.

Abbreviations

tsp = teaspoon
dessp = dessertspoon
tbsp = tablespoon
oz = ounce
g = gram
lb = pound
mls = millilitres
kg = kilogram
fl. oz = fluid ounce

Weights and Measures

1 ounce = 25 grammes, approximately
1 lb = 450 grammes, approximately
2¼ lbs = 1 kilogramme approximately
¼ pint = 5 fluid ounces or 1 gill
1¾ pints = 1 litre

HANDY HINTS AND TIPS

Test for hot fat or oil for shallow or deep frying
Heat fat until you think it is almost hot enough. Dip the handle of a wooden spoon in the centre of the fat. When small bubbles appear round the handle the fat or oil is ready for use.

Crisp Roast Potatoes
Partly cook even size potatoes for about 3-4 minutes in salted boiling water. Drain well and toss in seasoned flour. Heat fat in roasting tin and then add the potatoes, basting well. This ensures a crisp, but not tough result.

Crunchy Crackling
Rub the scored pork skin with oil or lard and sprinkle with salt and dry mustard if liked. Roast at fairly high temperature at the end of cooking time, if not for the whole cooking time.

Frying eggs

Melt a little bacon fat in frying pan, add eggs and cover with suitable lid. Cook about 1 minute and the yolks will be nicely covered with a white film.

Egg Whites

If egg whites have been stored and the number forgotten, each white of standard eggs (size 3) should weigh one ounce. So first weigh a bowl and then add the weight required.

Filling a large piping bag for cream, meringue or potato

Stand bag with tube in the end, inside a jar, jug or round grater. Fold back the top of the bag and fill with mixture. Turn up the edge and close ready for use.

Cleaning mustard and cress

Cut cress stalks and place cress in colander. Rinse well with cold water which should wash away seeds. Drain and use.

Grating orange or lemon rind

Use a medium grater and take care to grate the coloured zest only as the white pith is bitter. Use a pastry brush to remove the rind.

Percolating coffee

Rinse the coffee container (with perforations) in cold water before adding the coffee grains. This helps to prevent them falling in the water. Some people say a pinch of salt improves the flavour.

Gelatine

To dissolve gelatine successfully, put in a small basin with a little liquid. Stand in a saucepan with water coming halfway up. Heat gently until dissolved. $1/2$ oz gelatine will set 1 pint of liquid.

Bouquet Garni

This usually comprises a bay leaf, sprig of thyme, leaf of sage and a few parsley stalks tied together and removed at end of cooking. Sometimes a strip of lemon rind or piece of celery is included.

SOUPS, STARTERS AND SAVOURIES

Watercress is widely grown and is famous in Hampshire. It is full of food value and a colourful garnish for many savoury dishes and salads.

Watercress Soup

1 bunch watercress
1 small onion, chopped
1 oz (25g) butter or margarine
8 ozs (225g) potatoes, peeled and sliced
12½ fl. ozs (330mls) water
½ pint (275mls) milk
salt and pepper
1 tbsp cream

Method

Wash cress and remove coarse stalks.
Chop cress and cook gently with onion in melted butter or margarine until soft.
Add potatoes with water and cook until soft.
Sieve or blend.
Add milk and bring to boil.
Stir in cream and more seasoning.
Serve hot.

Watercress Stuffing (for lamb or chicken)

1 medium onion, chopped
2-3 sticks celery, chopped
2 ozs (50g) melted butter or margarine
1 tsp salt, little pepper
3 ozs (75g) watercress, chopped
5 ozs (150g) fresh breadcrumbs
1 egg and little milk

Method

Mix all ingredients together except egg and milk, making sure onion and celery are finely chopped.
Bind with beaten egg and milk.
Use as required.

Watercress Sauce

1 bunch watercress
½ pint (275mls) water or fish stock
1 oz (25g) butter or bacon fat
1 oz (25g) flour
salt and pepper
1 tbsp cream

Method

Strip leaves from cress and chop stalks.
Boil leaves and stalks in stock or water until just soft.
Drain and chop finely.
Melt fat, add flour and cook few minutes.
Add strained liquor gradually to make sauce.
Bring to boil and season. Add cress and cream. Serve hot.

Hampshire Cottage Broth

This is a very old Hampshire recipe sent from Australia. Be warned – it takes a long time to complete!

1 sheep's head with salted water to cover
1 dessp salt
1 onion, 1 turnip
2 carrots, 2 sticks celery
2 leeks
1 bay leaf and sprig parsley
2 ozs (50g) pearl barley
salt and pepper

Method

Remove brains and tongue.
Soak head in salt water for 8 hours, changing water about every hour.
Scrape small bones from nostrils, wash head and place in pan with 1 dessp salt. Cover with cold water and bring to boil.
Remove and rinse well.
Dice vegetables and rinse barley in cold water.
Put head in pan, add 6 pints water.
Add barley and tongue.
Bring to boil, skim, add seasoning. Simmer 3 hours.
Add vegetables, bay leaf and parsley. Simmer 15 minutes.
Remove head.
Simmer broth 1/2 hour. Add diced meat.

The next two recipes come from an old edition of Farmhouse Fare.

Rabbit Paste – a tasty type of pâté or spread with a mild flavour

1 rabbit, in small joints
2 ozs (50g) butter or margarine
1 tsp sugar
12 allspice, 6 peppercorns
3 blades mace
1 onion, stuck with 12 cloves
8 ozs (225g) butter
1 dessp Worcester sauce
pinch cayenne pepper
1 tsp sugar
small dishes or ramekins

Method

Place rabbit joints in casserole with 2 ozs (50g) butter or margarine, peppercorns, allspice, sugar and onion.
Cover closely and cook slowly until meat leaves bones, Gas 3, 325°F, 170°C about 1 hour.
Mince meat finely or blend.
Beat in butter, Worcester sauce, sugar and cayenne pepper.
Press into dishes. Serve on hot toast.

Onion Toast

2 large Spanish onions
1 oz (25g) butter
4 slices hot buttered toast
salt and pepper
4 slices Cheddar cheese
made mustard

Method

Fry onion in rings in melted butter until brown.
Spread thickly on buttered toast and season.
Cover with thin slices of cheese and spread with mustard.
Grill until cheese is melted.

Pig's Head Cheese

Another old Hampshire recipe from Australia which can be served as a savoury or with salad.

1 pig's head, cleaned
salt and pepper
mace and nutmeg
dried sage

Method

Cover head with boiling water and leave 2 minutes.
Drain and place in pan.
Cover with boiling water again and bring back to boil.
Simmer until tender, removing scum.
Bone and chop or mince meat.
Add seasoning and sage.
Line colander with muslin and drain meat.
Cover with muslin and weights. Press 12 hours.

MEAT DISHES AND MAIN COURSES

Pig farming has been widespread in Hampshire for centuries. A number of recipes using all parts of the animal have therefore been included.

Mrs. Beeton wrote "There is no domestic animal so profitable or useful to man as the pig, or any that yields him a more varied or luxurious repast." With the development of home freezers it is now possible to enjoy pork at any time of year, not just when there is an 'r' in the month. The whole pig carcase is suitable for roasting. The flesh should be smooth and firm and cut surfaces should be slightly moist, not wet. Flesh should be pink and fat, white and firm.

The most famous Hampshire recipe is:

Hampshire Haslet

8 ozs (225g) stale white bread
2 lbs (900g) fairly lean pork, minced
1 small onion, chopped
1 tsp salt and 1/2 tsp pepper
1 tsp sage
large greased loaf tin

Method

Cut bread into cubes and soak in milk or water to cover.
When soft, squeeze out excess moisture and add bread to meat, onion, sage and seasoning.
Mince all together or blend.
Shape into oblongs and fill greased tin.
Bake gas 5, 375°F, 190°C about 1 1/2 hours or well done.

Pork or Lamb Fingers

A very economical recipe using belly of pork or breast of lamb.

1 lb (450g) belly pork or 1 breast of lamb
1 small onion and carrot
1 stick celery
few parsley stalks
pinch dried mixed herbs
salt and pepper
1 beaten egg
fresh breadcrumbs
seasoned flour
oil or lard for frying
to serve – mashed potato, carrots and peas

Method

Cover meat, onion, carrot, celery, herbs and seasoning with water and bring to boil, skim and cook until tender.
Remove bones and press meat between plates overnight.
Remove excess fat and cut meat into fingers. Toss in seasoned flour, then in egg and breadcrumbs.
Fry in shallow oil or lard until crisp and brown.
Make mound of mashed potato in centre of dish.
Prop fingers of meat round and add peas and carrots.

Pork and Apple Pie

A tasty pie with a covering of pastry or mashed potato.

1 lb (450g) lean pork
2 onions, sliced
2 cooking apples, sliced thinly
2 lbs (900g) potatoes, sliced thinly
1 tsp chopped fresh sage
1 oz (25g) lard or dripping
1/4 pt (150mls) stock
salt and pepper
8 ozs (225g) shortcrust pastry
or mashed potato topping

Method

Cut pork in small pieces and season.
Place in dish in layers with apples, onions and potatoes, sprinkling with sage and seasoning.
Dot with fat and cover.
Cook 1 1/2 hours gas 3, 325°F, 170°C.
Cool and cover with pastry or mashed potato.
Bake 1/2 hour gas 7, 425°F, 220°C.

Pork Orange Mould

A very tasty brawn to serve with salad.

1 lb (450g) shoulder of pork, cut small
¼ pint (150mls) orange juice from a large orange
grated rind of 1 orange
sprig of rosemary
bay leaf and 8 peppercorns
pinch ground ginger
salt and pepper
1 pint (575mls) water
1 oz (25g) gelatine or 1 pig's trotter

Method

Put pork in pan with water and trotter (if used) and bring to boil.
Skim and add rest of ingredients except gelatine.
Simmer until tender.
Remove bay leaf, rosemary and peppercorns.
Dissolve gelatine in a little cooking liquor and stir in.
(Using a trotter will set the mould). Put in wet mould and set.

Shiver of Pork

3 lbs (1.5kg) top leg of pork
oil, salt
4 cooking apples, quartered
4 onions, halved
4 potatoes, parboiled

Method

Score skin of pork in narrow strips and brush with oil and rub with salt.
Bake at gas 5, 375°F, 190°C, for 40 minutes.
Add apples, onions and potatoes round joint in tin.
Cook about 1½ hours until well done.

Crown of Pork

1 pork loin (12 rib bones) chined
oil and salt
sage and onion stuffing
4 large onions, parboiled and chopped
4 ozs (110g) breadcrumbs
2 tsps sage
1½ ozs (40g) suet
salt and pepper
beaten egg to bind
1 large cooking apple, chopped
12 small onions
cutlet frills and cocktail sticks

Method

Score skin of pork finely.
Rub with oil and salt.
Mix stuffing ingredients and bind with egg.
Form meat into a circle and skewer into crown shape.
Cut 1½ inches down between each chop.
Tie with string. Put in tin and fill centre with stuffing and chopped apple.
Roast 30 minutes to the pound plus 30 minutes at gas 6, 400°F, 200°C.
Add onions round meat for last hour.
Remove skewers and string.
Add frills on sticks.

Two recipes using pig's liver from 'Farmhouse Fare'. If the flavour of pig's liver is rather strong, soak it in milk and water for an hour, then drain and use.

Faggot Loaves

2 eggs
2 tbsps flour
¼ pint (150mls) milk
salt and pepper
1 tsp mixed dried herbs
8 ozs (225g) pig's liver
2 medium onions
2 rashers bacon
2-3 slices bread
small oven dishes

Method

Make a thick batter with beaten eggs, milk and flour.
Add herbs and seasoning.
Mince liver, onions and bacon.
Soak bread in a little milk and mix with liver etc.
Bind well with batter.
Put in greased pots and stand in pan of water to come halfway and bake 45 minutes, gas 7, 425°F, 220°C.

Liver Puffs

4 ozs (110g) pig's liver
water to cover
3 ozs (75g) macaroni or rice
½ oz (15g) butter
1 tbsp flour
¼ pint (150mls) milk
2 eggs, beaten
1 tbsp chopped parsley
oil for deep frying

Method

Parboil liver in water to cover for 5 minutes.
Cook macaroni or rice in boiling water about 9 minutes.
Mince or chop liver and macaroni.
Melt butter, stir in flour and cook few minutes until light brown.
Add milk and stir until thick.
Add liver, macaroni or rice and parsley.
Heat through and bind with egg.
Drop large spoonsful into hot oil and cook until puffed up.
Makes about 12.

Pig's Head Brawn (an old recipe)

Brine

6 pints (3½ litres) cold water
8 ozs (225g) cooking salt
¼ oz (8g) salt petre (optional)
½ pig's head
1-2 pig's trotters
pinch ground ginger, pepper and nutmeg
large basin or mould

Method

Mix brine ingredients.
Add an egg which should float slowly to top. If it rises too quickly add more water to brine.
Soak head and trotters in brine for 3 days. Drain and rinse well.
Cook almost covered in fresh water about 2 hours.
Cut meat in small pieces and skim fat off stock.
Strain some stock into pan, add meat and seasoning and bring to boil.
Fill wetted mould and press until cold.

Hampshire Savoury Roll

6 tbsps milk
I tbsp semolina or ground rice
I lb (450g) mashed potatoes
I tbsp chopped parsley
2 tbsps grated raw carrot
2 tbsps cooked bacon or ham, chopped
3 ozs (75g) grated Cheddar cheese
I tsp yeast extract
seasoning, parsley
browned breadcrumbs

Method

Boil milk and stir in semolina or rice. Boil until really thick.
Add other ingredients and form into roll.
Coat with breadcrumbs and bake in greased tin gas 7, 425°F, 220°C for 20 minutes.
Serve garnished with parsley.

Buried Treasure

I¹/2 lbs (675g) sliced carrots
I oz (25g) butter or bacon fat
I onion, chopped
8 ozs (225g) lean bacon, cut small
I tbsp sugar, salt and pepper
8 large prunes, pre-soaked
I tbsp flour
¹/4 pint (150mls) milk

Method

Melt fat and cook carrots and onion gently without colouring.
Add bacon pieces with sugar and seasoning.
Blend flour with milk and mix in.
Put in casserole and bury the prunes.
Bake covered gas 5, 375°F, 190°C for I¹/2 hours.

Meon Valley Meat Loaf

I lb (450g) cooked bacon or ham
I lb (450g) lean minced beef
¹/4 large loaf in breadcrumbs
¹/2 tsp nutmeg
seasoning and pinch of herbs
I large egg
browned crumbs

Method

Mix meats and breadcrumbs with seasoning, nutmeg and herbs.
Bind with beaten egg.
Fill greased pudding basin.
Cover and steam for I¹/2 hours.
Remove cover and leave over water for 10 minutes.
Turn out and cover with browned crumbs.
Serve with gravy or sauce.

Gammon and Cider

4 gammon steaks
3 tsps mustard
3 tsps demerara sugar
1 tbsp cornflour
1/2 pint (275mls) cider
2 tbsps cream
chopped parsley

Method

Soak gammon 1/2 hour. Dry and remove rinds.
Make paste with mustard, sugar and a little cider.
Place gammon in casserole and spread with paste.
Leave for 15 minutes.
Pour over rest of cider, cover and bake gas 6, 400°F, 200°C for 30 minutes.
Drain liquor into pan and thicken with blended cornflour.
Season and add cream, then pour over gammon and garnish with parsley.

Hampshire Bacon and Onion Roll

An economical and filling dish making good use of bacon off-cuts.

8 ozs (225g) self-raising flour
4 ozs (110g) shredded suet, pinch salt
cold water to mix
6 ozs (175g) bacon pieces, chopped
2 onions, thinly sliced
2 tbsps chopped parsley
pepper

Method

Mix suet with flour and salt.
Add enough water to make soft dough and roll to oblong.
Cover with bacon and onion.
Sprinkle with parsley and pepper.
Roll up and wrap loosely in foil.
Steam 2-2 1/2 hours. Serve hot with gravy.

Keeper's Pie

1 rabbit, jointed
seasoned flour
2 ozs (50g) bacon pieces
3 onions, sliced
seasoning
sprig parsley, blade of mace
1 pint (575mls) stock
4 ozs (110g) pickled pork, chopped
1 oz (25g) butter
1oz (25g) flour

Method

Rinse, drain and dry rabbit joints.
Dip in seasoned flour.
Place half of bacon in casserole, add rabbit and onions.
Add stock, herbs and pork.
Cover with rest of bacon.
Cook covered until tender gas 5, 375°F, 190°C about 1 1/2 hours.
Strain and skim liquor.
Melt butter, add flour and cook few minutes.
Add liquor gradually to make sauce.
Bring to boil and pour over rabbit.

South Down Dumplings

8 ozs (225g) plain flour
1 tsp salt
2 tsps baking powder
1/2 tsp curry powder
2 ozs (50g) butter
1 lb (450g) boiled chicken or rabbit, chopped
milk
stock from meat
2 tbsps chopped parsley

Method

Sieve flour, baking powder and salt.
Stir in curry powder and rub in butter.
Add chopped meat and mix with milk to a thick batter.
Form into small dumplings.
Bring stock to boil and drop in dumplings and cook about 12 minutes.
Drain and serve with parsley.

Rabbit and Trotter Brawn

1 rabbit, jointed
2 pigs' trotters
1 large onion
1 tbsp chopped parsley
seasoning

Method

Cover trotters with cold water and cook 1 1/2 hours.
Add rabbit joints, onion, parsley and seasoning.
Cook further 2 hours.
Strain and remove meat from bones.
Cut meat in small pieces and cover with liquor in basin.
Leave to set about 24 hours.

Pheasant with Apples

1 young pheasant
4 ozs (110g) butter
8 medium cooking apples, sliced
1 oz (25g) sugar
3 tbsps cream
1 bayleaf, seasoning
1 oz (25g) breadcrumbs
watercress

Method

Wipe pheasant. Melt 3 ozs (75g) butter in heavy pan and brown bird all over.
Put apple slices in casserole with rest of butter.
Sprinkle with sugar and cook gently until apples are softening.
Place bird on top and pour over juices from pan.
Add bay leaf and seasoning and pour cream over breast.
Cover and cook gas 4, 350°F, 180°C for 3/4-1 hour.
Serve sprinkled with breadcrumbs. Add watercress.

Skimmer Dick

A very old, simple country recipe.
While a joint of bacon is boiling, add a dough of self-raising flour, salt and water to cover the bacon and surround it with cabbage.

14

SUPPER SNACKS

Surprise Savoury Potatoes

4 large potatoes, scrubbed
4 lambs' kidneys, with fat round
seasoning
butter

Method

Cut potatoes in half and hollow out centres.
Fit in kidneys with fat round or spread with butter.
Fit halves together and wrap in buttered foil.
Bake gas 2, 300°F, 150°C for about 2 hours.

Hampshire Onions

4 large onions
4 lambs' kidneys with fat
seasoning

Method

Cook onions 15 minutes in boiling water.
Hollow out tops carefully and put kidney with fat in top of each.
Roast gas 3, 325°F, 170°C until tender.

Fried Marrow with poached eggs

1 marrow, peeled
flour
1 beaten egg
white breadcrumbs
oil or lard
4 eggs

Variation

4 ozs (110g) batter
fried bacon rashers

Method

Remove seeds from marrow and cut in $1/2''$ slices.
Dip in flour and brush with egg.
Dip in breadcrumbs, then fry in hot oil or lard until golden.
Keep hot while eggs are poached.
Place on top of marrow.
Variation – dip marrow slices in thick batter with bacon (chopped). Fry in oil.

Shanklin Eggs

4 hard boiled eggs
8 olives
4 red chillies
8 slices fried bread

Method

Halve eggs longways and remove yolks.
Sieve yolks and mix with finely chopped olives and chillies or use blender.
Add salt to taste and pipe into egg halves.
Place on fried bread slices. Serve cold.

FISH DISHES

Hampshire Haddock

2 lbs (900g) fresh haddock in one piece
Forcemeat 1/4 pt (150mls) breadcrumbs
       1 tsp chopped parsley
       1/2 tsp chopped thyme
       2 ozs (50g) suet
       grated rind 1/2 lemon
       seasoning, pinch nutmeg
       1 egg, 3 tbsps milk
1 oz (25g) butter
Sauce head and fish trimmings
       1 pint cold water, 1/2 tsp salt
       2 strips pared lemon rind
       1 tbsp flour, pepper
       1/2 oz (15g) butter
       1 tbsp cream

Method

Remove head, tail, bones and fins and clean fish.
Mix all forcemeat ingredients and stuff fish.
Tie with string and put in deep well greased casserole.
Dot with butter and bake 3/4 hour gas 5, 375°F, 190°C.
Sauce – stew head and trimmings in water with salt and lemon rind for 1/2 hour. Strain and thicken with flour and water paste.
Simmer 8 minutes then whisk in butter gradually.
Add pepper
Add cream just before serving.

Sparsholt Smokie

8 ozs (225g) smoked haddock
1 bay leaf
1 oz (25g) butter
1 oz (25g) flour
3 ozs (75g) Cheddar cheese
1/4 pint (150mls) dry cider
black pepper
grated Parmesan cheese
brown bread triangles

Method

Poach fish in 3/4 pint (425mls) water with bay leaf.
Melt butter and add flour.
Cook 2-3 minutes, then gradually add 1/2 pint (275mls) fish stock.
Bring to boil and simmer for 15 minutes.
Add 3 ozs (75g) cheese, pepper and cider.
Cook until thick and smooth.
Add flaked fish and divide between 4 oven dishes.
Sprinkle with Parmesan cheese and grill or bake until brown.
Serve with bread triangles.

PUDDINGS, SWEETS AND PRESERVES

Hampshire is famous for its delicious strawberries.

Real Strawberries and cream

A mixing bowl half full of lightly whipped double cream. Add as many strawberries as the bowl and cream will hold. Stir gently, mashing slightly. When cream will not take any more fruit, leave bowl to stand one hour. Dredge with caster sugar. Serve on the lawn on a hot summer's day. Delicious!

Strawberry Shortcake

A one layer shortcake which is easy to serve and looks wonderful.

Method

10 ozs (275g) plain flour
5 ozs (150g) caster sugar
6 ozs (175g) butter
I egg
I lb (450g) strawberries
1/2 pint (275mls) cream, whipped
caster sugar
8″ flan tin

Mix flour and sugar. Rub in butter finely.
Mix with beaten egg and knead lightly.
Press into large flan or sandwich tin and prick with fork.
Bake gas 4, 350°F, 180°C for 35-40 minutes.
Remove from tin and cool.
Spread with some cream.
Cover with fruit.
Pipe border of cream and dust fruit with sugar.

Strawberry Cup

A delicious and refreshing fruit cup to serve at a summer garden party.

Method

strawberries
white sugar
water
I tsp brandy or kirsch to every 2 pints (1 1/4 litres) pulp
juice and rind I lemon
ice cubes

Mash strawberries and sieve.
Add I tsp brandy or kirsch to every 2 pints of pulp and leave 1/2 hour.
Add 2 pints of water with 6 ozs (175g) sugar and rind and juice of lemon to every 2 pints.
Stir until dissolved.
Strain and serve with ice cubes in glass jug.

Strawberry Conserve

This method keeps the fruit whole but takes longer, than jam.

Method

4 lbs (1.8kg) hulled strawberries
4 lbs (1.8kg) sugar

Put fruit in bowl with layers of sugar.
Leave 24 hours, then put in preserving pan and boil 5 minutes.
Return to bowl and leave 48 hours.
Place in pan again and boil 15-20 minutes until set.
Cool slightly before potting. Cover.

Blackberry Mould

1 lb (450g) blackberries
water to cover
³/₄ oz (25g) gelatine
¹/₂ pint (275mls) milk
3 dessps water
2-3 tbsps sugar
rinsed jelly mould

Method

Simmer fruit just covered with water until all juice is extracted. Strain.
Soak gelatine in 3 dessps water.
To ¹/₂ pint (275mls) juice add ¹/₂ pint (275mls) milk,
Heat with sugar to blood heat.
Add dissolved gelatine and stir until it curdles without boiling.
Pour into mould to set.
When turned out, clear jelly will be on top.

Rhubarb Stirabout

The original recipe did not include an egg, but the addition of an egg makes a better batter.

4 ozs (110g) plain flour
2 ozs (50g) margarine
1 egg, 5 tbsps milk
8 ozs (225g) rhubarb cut in 1″ pieces
2 ozs (50g) caster sugar
golden syrup

Method

Rub margarine into flour finely.
Add beaten egg and milk.
Stir in sugar and rhubarb.
Pour into greased pie dish and bake gas 7, 425°F, 220°C for 35-40 minutes.
Pour over syrup while hot.

Bournemouth Pudding

A steamed ginger pudding for a cold winter's day.

5 ozs (150g) fresh breadcrumbs
3 ozs (75g) suet
1 heaped tsp ground ginger
or 2 ozs (50g) chopped ginger
¹/₂ tsp bicarbonate soda
1 beaten egg
2 tbsps milk
2 tbsps golden syrup
Sauce 2 tbsps syrup
juice ¹/₂ lemon

Method

Mix breadcrumbs, suet, ginger and soda together.
Add beaten egg, milk and syrup.
Steam in greased basin 2 hours.
Sauce – heat syrup and lemon juice.

Bay Rice

An old Hampshire way to flavour a rice pudding.

The pudding is mixed in the usual way but ground cloves and bay leaves cover the top and then mixed spice is sprinkled over. The proportion of milk should be reduced to make a thick pudding which is served in slices.

Apple Bread Pudding

Just a variation of bread pudding with the added flavour of apples.

Method

bread slices, well buttered
slivers of stewed apple, sweetened
sultanas
buttered pie dish

Put layers of apple between slices of bread with sultanas.
Dot top with more sultanas and apples.
Bake until crisp on top.
Serve cold cut in slices.

Friar's Omelette

Similar to an apple charlotte but nothing like an omelette.

Method

6 good sized cooking apples
3 ozs (75g) butter
2 ozs (50g) caster sugar
grated rind 1 lemon
pinch nutmeg or cloves
3-4 ozs (75-110g) breadcrumbs
4 egg yolks
extra butter

Bake apples in skins until soft.
Scrape out pulp.
Cream butter and sugar.
Add lemon rind with apple pulp and nutmeg.
Sprinkle greased pie dish with good layer of crumbs.
Beat yolks and add to apple mix.
Pour into dish and cover with rest of crumbs.
Dot with butter and bake gas 5, 375°F, 190°C for ¾ hour until set.

Cowes Pudding

Method

½ oz (15g) butter
2 eggs
2 tbsps caster sugar
½ pint (275g) milk
4 ozs (110g) sponge fingers
2ozs (50g) blanched almonds
few drops almond essence
Sauce 3 egg yolks
    1 tbsp caster sugar
    ¼ pint (150mls) sherry
    2 drops almond essence

Grease basin with butter.
Beat eggs with sugar.
Warm milk and pour on to egg mix.
Strain into double pan or basin over hot water and cook custard until it coats back of wooden spoon.
Line basin with sponge fingers.
Add chopped nuts and essence to custard.
Pour into basin, cover and steam ¾ hour.
Stand 1 minute before turning out.
Sauce – whisk yolks, sugar, sherry and essence until thick over water.

Vectis Pudding (Isle of Wight)

8 ozs (225g) self-raising flour
4 ozs (110g) suet
2 ozs (50g) currants
2 chopped cooking apples
3 tbsps golden syrup
2ozs (50g) sugar
grated rind 1/2 lemon
pinch mixed spice

Method

Make a stiff dough with flour, suet and water.
Roll thinly and spread with fruit, syrup, lemon rind and spice.
Roll up, closing dampened ends firmly
Wrap loosely in greased foil and steam 2 hours.

Sandown Pudding

A simple form of charlotte russe.

sponge fingers or boudoir biscuits
2 ozs (50g) halved glacé cherries
2 ozs (50g) ratafias
1 pint (575mls) custard
1 oz (25g) gelatine, dissolved in a little water
whipped cream

Method

Line tin or mould with sponge fingers or boudoir biscuits.
Add cherries and ratafias.
Add dissolved gelatine to warmed custard and mix well before pouring into mould.
Leave to set, then turn out and decorate with cream.

Frumerty

A very old Hampshire dish similar to the modern muesli. In the old days wheat grains were gleaned in the cornfields at harvest time.

wheat grains
milk
sultanas or chopped fruit
brown sugar to taste
chopped nuts
cream

Method

Soak wheat grains in milk until soft.
Boil until milk is taken up.
Add sultanas during cooking and fresh fruit when serving.
Dip cut apples, pears and bananas in lemon juice.
Add sugar and nuts.
Serve with cream.

Isle of Wight Pies

A Hampshire version of the old fashioned cheese cakes.

8 ozs (225g) plain flour
2 ozs (50g) margarine
2ozs (50g) lard
water to mix
} pastry

2 eggs
4 ozs (110g) caster sugar
4 ozs (110g) butter, 2 large tbsps ground rice
1/2 tsp nutmeg, glacé cherries, halved

Method

Make pastry and line patty tins.
Beat eggs and sugar until thick.
Soften butter and beat in with rice and nutmeg.
Half fill tins.
Place cherry halves on top.
Bake gas 5, 375°F, 190°C 15-20 minutes until brown.

Hampshire Pie

A Hampshire version of a bakewell tart.

6 ozs (175g) puff or shortcrust pastry
3-4 tbsps raspberry or apricot jam
3 ozs (75g) butter
3 egg yolks and 2 egg whites
3 ozs (75g) caster sugar
deep 8" (20cm) pie plate or flan

Method

Line plate or flan with pastry and prick base. Spread with jam.
Soften butter.
Whisk yolks and sugar until thick.
Whisk in butter gradually.
Whisk egg whites until stiff and fold in.
Pour into case. Bake gas 6, 400°F, 200°C, for 1/2 hour.

Grannie's Christmas Pudding

More breadcrumbs and less flour makes this pudding lighter in texture without detracting from the flavour and colour.

1 lb (450g) finely chopped beef suet (fresh from
 butcher if possible)
1 lb (450g) fresh breadcrumbs
1 lb (450g) dark brown sugar
1 lb (450g) each of sultanas, currants and raisins
1 lb (450g) chopped candied peel
4 ozs (110g) ground almonds
5 ozs (150g) plain flour
1/2 oz (15g) mixed spice
1 tsp ground nutmeg
1/2 tsp salt
rind and juice 2 lemons
6 eggs
1/4 pint (150mls) rum
1/8 pint (75mls) brandy
small glass stout or ale

Method

Mix all dry ingredients well.
Beat eggs and stir in with all liquids.
Threequarters fill 6 medium greased pudding basins.
Cover and steam 6 hours.
Cool and re-cover with greaseproof paper.
Boil or steam for 3 hours before serving.
Avoid covering with foil for storing as this could cause mould.

Apricot and Pineapple Jam

1 lb (450g) dried apricots
1 large tin pineapple pieces
3 pints (1.75 litres) water
3 lbs sugar

Method

Wash dried fruit well and cut finely.
Add to pineapple, cover with water and pineapple juice and soak 24 hours.
Bring to boil gently in buttered preserving pan.
Boil 20 minutes.
Add sugar and boil 8-10 minutes. Test for set and fill jars. Cover when cold.

Delicious Sweet Chutney

1 lb (450g) dates, chopped
3 lbs (1.35kg) cooking apples, peeled and chopped
8 ozs (225g) brown sugar
2 pints (1.25 litres) malt vinegar
1 lb (450g) onions, chopped
2 ozs (50g) ground ginger
pinch cayenne
pinch ground cloves

Method

Mix all ingredients together in pan and boil 1 hour until thick.
Pot when cool.

Pickled Green Cabbage

1 large cabbage
4 large onions
salt
2 pints (1.25 litres) malt vinegar
8 ozs (225g) flour
1 lb (450g) sugar
2 tsps curry powder
2 tbsps dry mustard
1 pint (575mls) vinegar

Method

Shred cabbage finely.
Add to finely chopped onions.
Put in bowl, sprinkle with salt and leave 24 hours.
Drain well and boil slowly in 2 pints (1.25 litres) vinegar 20 minutes.
Mix flour, sugar, curry powder and mustard in other pint (575mls) vinegar.
Pour over cabbage and boil 5 minutes.
Pot while hot.

Hedgerow Jelly

3 lbs (1.35kg) crab apples or windfall cooking apples
3 lbs (1.35kg) blackberries
3 lbs (1.35kg) mixed sloes, elderberries, rosehips
1 lb (450g) sugar to each pint (575mls) juice
jelly bag

Method

Wash and cut up apples and cover with water.
Boil until soft.
Strain through jelly bag.
Cook berries and other fruit in same way after removing stems, pricking sloes, topping and tailing hips.
Strain as above and mix juices together.
Add sugar and cook gently to dissolve, then boil until set.

22

CAKES AND BISCUITS

Hampshire Lardy Cakes are famous and traditionally do not include fruit. The secret of a good lardy cake is to turn it upside down after baking so that the lard can soak through.

Lardy Cake

1 lb (450g) risen bread dough
8 ozs (225g) sugar
8 ozs (225g) lard
pinch salt
optional – 3 ozs (75g) sultanas

Method

Roll dough as thinly as possible into oblong on well floured board.
Spread with one-fifth of lard, sugar and fruit, if used.
Fold into 3 and roll again (like puff pastry).
Repeat layers 4 times, then fold into 3 and flatten to make oblong.
Sprinkle with sugar. Prove on warm tin, then cook gas 7, 425°F, 220°C about 45 minutes. Reverse on cooling tray.

Isle of Wight Doughnuts

2 ozs (50g) butter
1/2 oz (15g) fresh yeast
1 lb (450g) flour
1/2 tsp salt
1 oz (25g) sugar
71/2 fl. ozs (225mls) milk
2 eggs
raspberry jam
oil for frying

Method

Mix flour, salt and sugar.
Divide equally in 2 basins.
Rub butter into 1, and mix yeast and milk into other.
Let this rise 1/2 hour, then mix both together and beat in eggs.
Knead and divide into 24 pieces.
Shape into balls.
Make hole in each and add little jam.
Close up using egg to seal.
Prove 10 minutes.
Drop 4-5 at a time in boiling oil and cook until golden.
Drain and toss in caster sugar.

Farmhouse Wholemeal Bread

2 lbs (900g) wholemeal flour
1 tbsp salt
1 oz (25g) fresh yeast
1 tbsp black treacle
11/4 pints (725mls) lukewarm water
2 loaf tins

Method

Mix flour and salt in warm bowl.
Cream yeast with treacle and water.
Pour into flour, mix and knead for 5 minutes.
Shape into two loaves and put in greased tins.
Put to rise about 45 minutes.
Bake gas 7, 425°F, 220°C for 25 minutes.
Reduce to gas 6, 400°F, 200°C for 10 minutes. Turn out to cool.

Note – Easy Blend yeast may be used. Omit treacle and mix yeast dry with flour before adding water.

Gipsy Bread

This is a dark teabread without yeast.

10 ozs (275g) self-raising flour
pinch salt and mixed spice
4 ozs (110g) soft brown sugar
6 ozs (175g) sultanas
1 tbsp milk
6 ozs (175g) black treacle
2 ozs (50g) chopped peel
1 egg
1/4 tsp bicarbonate of soda
2 tsps milk
2 lb (900g) loaf tin, greased

Method

Mix dry ingredients.
Warm treacle with milk.
Whisk in egg.
Dissolve soda in milk and add to mix.
Mix and pour into tin.
Bake gas 4, 350°F, 180°C for 45 minutes.
Reduce to gas 3, 325°F, 170°C for 30 minutes. Cool in tin 10 minutes.
Slice and spread with butter.

Very Dark Gingerbread

4 ozs (110g) margarine
4 ozs (110g) soft brown sugar
4 ozs (110g) black treacle
6 ozs (175g) plain flour
level tsp ground ginger
level tsp cinnamon
1 egg
1/4 pint (150mls) milk
level tsp bicarbonate of soda
square tin

Method

Grease and line base of square tin.
Melt margarine, sugar and treacle without boiling.
Sieve flour, ginger and cinnamon together.
Stir in melted mix and add beaten egg.
Add slightly warm milk to soda and stir in.
Beat well and pour batter into tin.
Bake gas 2, 300°F, 150°C about 1 hour.
Turn out and cool.
Keep several days before eating.

Isle of Wight Farmhouse Fruit Cake

8 ozs (225g) butter, margarine or dripping
1 lb (450g) plain flour
8 ozs (225g) sugar
1/2 tsp spice, pinch salt
1/2 tsp bicarbonate soda
1/2 pint (275mls) warm milk
8 ozs (225g) each, currants, raisins and sultanas
2 ozs (50g) chopped peel
1 large egg
greased bread tin

Method

Rub fat into flour finely.
Add sugar, spice, salt and fruit.
Make well in centre and add soda and milk with beaten egg.
Mix to dough and put in well greased tin.
Add slice of peel on top and bake gas 4, 350°F, 180°C about 1 1/2 hours.

New Forest Gâteau

Red cherries and an easy chocolate cake mixture make this a gorgeous gâteau.

5 ozs (150g) self-raising flour
6 ozs (175g) caster sugar
6 ozs (175g) soft margarine
3 ozs (75g) drinking chocolate
3 eggs (size 3)
3 tbsps boiling water

Filling and decoration

large tin red cherries, stoned
4 ozs (110g) sugar
4 tbsps water
4 tbsps kirsch
1 pint (575mls) double cream
two 7" sandwich tins, greased and floured
chocolate strands

Method

Beat all cake ingredients well to a smooth batter.
Bake in two tins gas 4, 350°F, 180°C for 1/2 hour.
Leave for 5 minutes, then turn out.
Drain cherries. Bring juice to boil in pan with water and sugar and boil 2 minutes without stirring.
Cool and add most of kirsch.
Prick cakes and pour over syrup.
Whip cream and fold in rest of kirsch.
Spread some on one cake.
Add most of the cherries.
Cover with other cake.
Spread sides with cream and roll in chocolate strands.
Spread cream on top and decorate with cherries and piped cream.

Honey Nut Tartlets (12)

8 ozs (225g) flour, pinch salt
5 ozs (150g) butter or margarine
1 egg
3 tbsps milk
2 tbsps honey
2 ozs (50g) minced walnuts
2 ozs (50g) caster sugar

Method

Rub fat into flour and salt.
Make dough with beaten egg and milk.
Chill 20 minutes. Roll out and line bun tins.
Mix honey, nuts and sugar.
Threequarters fill pastry cases.
Bake gas 6, 400°F, 200°C, about 20 minutes until brown.

Hampshire Honey Knobs (36)

8 ozs (225g) plain flour
1/4 tsp salt
1 tsp baking powder
1 tsp cinnamon
5 ozs (150g) butter
4 ozs (110g) brown sugar
3 ozs (75g) honey
4 ozs (110g) raisins
3 ozs (75g) bran
3/4 tsp bicarbonate soda
1/4 pint (150mls) milk
2 ozs (50g) chopped nuts
2 eggs

Method

Sieve flour, baking powder, cinnamon and salt.
Melt butter, add sugar, honey and beaten eggs and mix well.
Dissolve soda in milk and add alternately with dry ingredients.
Stir in raisins, nuts and bran.
Drop teaspoonsful on greased baking trays.
Bake gas 5, 375°F, 190°C about 15 minutes.

Flapjacks

6 ozs (175g) margarine
2 ozs (50g) sugar
1 tbsp golden syrup
8 ozs (225g) porridge oats
few drops vanilla essence

Method

Melt margarine, sugar and syrup without boiling.
Stir in oats and essence and mix well.
Spread on greased swiss roll tin.
Bake gas 5, 375°F, 190°C, for 25 minutes.
Mark in pieces before turning out.

Hampshire Drops

4 ozs (110g) margarine
4 ozs (110g) caster sugar
1 egg, beaten
4 ozs (110g) self-raising flour
4 ozs (110g) cornflour
raspberry jam

Method

Cream margarine and sugar until pale.
Beat in egg and fold in mixed flours.
Put teaspoonsful well apart on greased baking tins.
Bake gas 4, 350°F, 180°C, for 10 minutes.
Cool and sandwich together with jam.

Gingerbread Husbands

A Hampshire speciality sold at Fairs. The gingerbread dough was pressed into wooden moulds, then baked and decorated.

1 lb (450g) plain flour
8 ozs (225g) soft brown sugar
1 tbsp ground ginger
8 ozs (225g) golden syrup
8 ozs (225g) margarine
currants and glacé cherries

Method

Mix flour, sugar and ginger.
Melt syrup and margarine without boiling.
Pour hot on to flour and stir to a paste. Leave to stand overnight.
Roll out and make gingerbread men.
Bake gas 3, 325°F, 170°C about 15 minutes until crisp.
Press on currants and cherries.

Some very old recipes

A Dish for Five Stout Men - Published 1772 exclusive

To nine pints of water one pound of lean beef cut into very thin pieces, 1 pint of split pease, 12 ounces of mealy potatoes, 3 ounces of ground rice after it has boiled 2 hours – 3 large leeks + 2 heads of cellery – twill cost a shilling exclusive of firing.

Short Bread

For short bread tak two pd of butter + rub it among a peck of flour + a muchken of good thik barm + clear watter: kned it up and roull out your kake + sie it get a slo or soft oven and let them not stay till they be burned.

From Your Corner Cupboard
Old Fashioned Sulphur Salve

Mix equal portions of home made lard and flowers of sulphur to a smooth paste. This very simple ointment is ready for use immediately and has been a wonderfully quick cure for most affections of the skin.

Tonic Stout

8 ozs (225g) black (or burnt) malt
1 oz (25g) hops
1 oz (25g) dried stinging nettles
1/4 oz (8g) black liquorice
2 medium potatoes
2 ozs (50g) brown sugar
1 oz (25g) yeast
10 pints water

Method

When water is at boiling point, add herbs, malt, hops, liquorice and potatoes (well washed but not peeled and pricked).
Simmer gently for 1 hour then strain into pan.
Add sugar. When about 95°F stir in yeast, which has been dissolved in a little warm liquid.
Cover up, stand for 24 hours, then skim off yeast and put in jar or bottles.
Cork lightly at first, tighten after 12 hours.
Leave 2 days. Beautiful creamy stout with remarkable tonic properties.

INDEX